The Words of
MARTIN LUTHER KING JR.

Jagger Youssef

PowerKiDS
press

Published in 2023 by The Rosen Publishing Group, Inc.
2544 Clinton Street, Buffalo, NY 14224

Copyright © 2023 by The Rosen Publishing Group, Inc.

All rights reserved. No part of this book may be reproduced in any form without permission in writing from the publisher, except by a reviewer.

Portions of this work were originally authored by Ryan Nagelhout and published as *Martin Luther King Jr. in His Own Words*. All new material in this edition authored by Jagger Youssef.

Editor: Therese Shea
Book Design: Michael Flynn

Photo Credits: Cover https://commons.wikimedia.org/wiki/File:Martin-Luther-King-1964-leaning-on-a-lectern.jpg; (series background) merrymuuu/Shutterstock.com; (fact box) Miloje/Shutterstock.com; pp. 5, 19 courtesy of the Library of Congress; p. 7 Alizada Studios/Shutterstock.com; p. 9 https://commons.wikimedia.org/wiki/File:MLK_statue,_Morehouse_College.jpg; p. 10 https://commons.wikimedia.org/wiki/File:Martin_Luther_King_Jr_NYWTS_5.jpg; p. 11 Mccallk69; p. 13 https://commons.wikimedia.org/wiki/File:Rosaparks.jpg; p. 14 Paolo Novello/Shutterstock.com; p. 15 Science History Images/Alamy Stock Photo; p. 17 https://commons.wikimedia.org/wiki/File:Civil_Rights_protesters_and_Woolworth%27s_Sit-In,_Durham,_NC,_10_February_1960._From_the_N%26O_Negative_Collection,_State_Archives_of_North_Carolina,_Raleigh,_NC._Photos_taken_by_The_News_%26_(24495308926).jpg; p. 18 https://commons.wikimedia.org/wiki/File:MLK_mugshot_birmingham.jpg; p. 20 https://commons.wikimedia.org/wiki/File:Martin_Luther_King_-_March_on_Washington.jpg; p. 21 Richard Cavalleri/Shutterstock.com; p. 23 https://commons.wikimedia.org/wiki/File:Martin_Luther_King_Jr_with_medallion_NYWTS.jpg; p. 25 https://en.wikipedia.org/wiki/File:Lyndon_Johnson_signing_Civil_Rights_Act,_July_2,_1964.jpg; p. 27 William Warren/Alamy Stock Photo.

Library of Congress Cataloging-in-Publication Data

Names: Youssef, Jagger, author.
Title: The words of Martin Luther King Jr. / Jagger Youssef.
Description: Buffalo, New York : PowerKids Press, [2023] | Series:
   Historical perspectives: in their own words | Includes index.
Identifiers: LCCN 2022027994 (print) | LCCN 2022027995 (ebook) | ISBN
   9781642824667 (library binding) | ISBN 9781642824643 (paperback) | ISBN
   9781642824674 (ebook)
Subjects: LCSH: King, Martin Luther, Jr., 1929-1968--Juvenile literature. |
   African Americans--Civil rights--Juvenile literature. | Civil rights
   movements--United States--History--20th century--Juvenile literature. |
   African Americans--Biography--Juvenile literature. | Civil rights
   workers--United States--Biography--Juvenile literature.
Classification: LCC E185.97.K5 Y68 2023 (print) | LCC E185.97.K5 (ebook)
   | DDC 323/.092 [B]--dc23/eng/20220613
LC record available at https://lccn.loc.gov/2022027994
LC ebook record available at https://lccn.loc.gov/2022027995

Manufactured in the United States of America

Some of the images in this book illustrate individuals who are models. The depictions do not imply actual situations or events.

CPSIA Compliance Information: Batch #CWPK23. For further information contact Rosen Publishing at 1-800-237-9932.

CONTENTS

A BORN LEADER

Martin Luther King Jr. was a leader of the U.S. civil rights movement in the 1950s and 1960s. His words and actions spurred on this movement and haven't been forgotten decades after his death.

King was born January 15, 1929, in Atlanta, Georgia. He was given the name Michael King Jr., after his father. His father, a Baptist minister, changed his own name to "Martin Luther King," after the religious figure Martin Luther. In 1934, Michael King Jr.'s name, too, was changed, to "Martin Luther King Jr."

The Kings, a middle-class family, lived in a home down the street from the Ebenezer Baptist Church, where King Sr. was the pastor and his father-in-law had been before that. Life was comfortable for the family, but they were constantly reminded they lived in a **segregated** society.

LOOKING BACK

This book uses Martin Luther King Jr.'s own words to help you understand more about his life and work.

Set in Stone

King grew up a short distance from Stone Mountain during a time when people were planning to carve images on the mountain honoring **Confederate** military leaders. The mountain would become a reminder of slavery and those who fought to keep it. Years later, King referred to Stone Mountain while calling for change on the steps of the Lincoln Memorial in one of the most famous speeches in American history. "Let freedom ring from Stone Mountain of Georgia," he said.

Martin Luther King Jr. was a powerful orator, or public speaker. His speeches moved people and called them to action.

5

SEGREGATION

The United States of Martin Luther King Jr.'s youth was divided by race. Although slavery officially ended in 1865 with the Thirteenth Amendment to the U.S. Constitution, Black Americans still weren't treated equally under the law. Segregation kept people separated, allowing "whites only" businesses, parks, schools, and even drinking fountains.

King's religious beliefs helped him realize early in his life that segregation and Jim Crow laws were unjust. In a sermon called "The Drum Major Instinct" delivered at Ebenezer Baptist Church in 1968, King said, "All men are brothers because they are children of a common father." He believed all people came from God and should be treated equally as peers.

LOOKING BACK

King grew up having white friends. One told him, when he was about 6, his parents wouldn't allow them to play together anymore—because of King's skin color.

A Life Apart

After the Thirteenth Amendment freed enslaved people in the United States, many states and cities passed laws to restrict the civil rights of Black Americans. Called Jim Crow laws, these measures made it hard for Black people to vote and segregated many areas of life. In Alabama, for example, Black and white people couldn't play pool together. (Jim Crow was a name for a character in minstrel shows, which featured white actors in dark makeup singing and dancing.)

King was born in this home on Auburn Avenue in Atlanta.

"INTELLIGENCE PLUS CHARACTER"

With a father and grandfather who were pastors, you might think Martin's future as a pastor was set in stone. However, as a student, he wasn't sure what he wanted to study. King went to Booker T. Washington High School, where he skipped the ninth and twelfth grades. At age 15, he began to attend Morehouse College in Atlanta. He hoped to study either law or medicine, but finally decided to become a minister. King said that at Morehouse he saw that a religious life could be "intellectually respectful and emotionally satisfying."

In his final year at Morehouse, King wrote about the nature of education in the school publication, *The Maroon Tiger:* "We must remember that intelligence is not enough. Intelligence plus character—that is the goal of true education."

LOOKING BACK

In 1943, King won an oratory contest. He and his teacher were made to give white people their bus seats and stand on the ride home, about 90 miles (145 km). "It was the angriest I have ever been in my life," he remembered.

Forming His Beliefs

Certain Morehouse College instructors influenced King's later beliefs and teachings. Morehouse president Dr. Benjamin E. Mays taught him about Mahatma Gandhi's nonviolent methods of protest against the British government in India. Professor Samuel W. Williams introduced him to Henry David Thoreau's "Essay on **Civil Disobedience**," which King read multiple times. King was fascinated by the idea of "refusing to cooperate with an evil system."

IN MEMORY OF
MARTIN LUTHER KING. JR. '48
1929 — 1968
OUTSTANDING ALUMNUS OF MOREHOUSE COLLEGE
WORLD-FAMOUS LEADER OF THE NON-VIOLENT MOVEMENT
DISTINGUISHED WINNER OF THE NOBEL PEACE PRIZE

From Morehouse College he launched his
humanitarian pilgrimage to create the
beloved community, and for that purpose
he moved out from the classroom and his
pulpit to march his way into immortality.

THIS STATUE IS A GIFT OF THE NATIONAL BAPTIST CONVENTION. U.S.A.,INC.
T. J. JEMISON, PRESIDENT
W. FRANKLYN RICHARDSON, GENERAL SECRETARY
MOREHOUSE COLLEGE

A statue of Martin Luther King Jr. is located on Morehouse campus next to the King Chapel. Morehouse is a historically Black college for men.

King gave his first sermon at the Ebenezer Baptist Church in 1947. He became a minister in 1948 at the age of 19 and graduated from Morehouse with a degree in **sociology**. He received a Bachelor of Divinity degree from Crozer Theological Seminary in Chester, Pennsylvania, in 1951. That September, King began his doctoral studies at Boston University, completing them in 1955.

Coretta Scott King

LOOKING BACK

Martin Luther King Jr. married Coretta Scott in 1953. They had four children together: Yolanda, Martin Luther King III, Dexter, and Bernice.

Calling for Change

King believed he could use his ministry as a call to action, to promote social change. He organized the Social and Political Action Committee within the Dexter Avenue Baptist Church. He wanted to make sure his church was informed about issues affecting their community and the nation. King believed people should always be ready to speak out and defend their civil rights. "The time is always right to do what's right," King later said.

King moved to Montgomery, Alabama, to become the pastor of Dexter Avenue Baptist Church. The five years he spent there would be active. He encouraged every member of the church to vote and to join the National Association for the Advancement of Colored People (NAACP), an organization that fights for Black Americans' rights.

King's church is now called the Dexter Avenue King Memorial Baptist Church. It's a National Historic Landmark.

THE MONTGOMERY BUS BOYCOTT

On December 1, 1955, a woman named Rosa Parks, on her way home from working in a Montgomery store, was ordered by a bus driver to give up her seat to a white passenger. She refused. Parks was arrested and sent to jail. Leaders of the NAACP, including King and chapter president Edgar Nixon, decided to use Parks's case to fight bus segregation in Montgomery.

"We have no alternative but to protest," King said four days after Parks was arrested. "For many years we have shown an amazing patience . . . But we come here tonight to be saved from that patience that makes us patient with anything less than freedom and justice." The newly formed Montgomery Improvement Association, led by King, made a **boycott** of the bus system their major goal.

LOOKING BACK

At the time of her arrest, Rosa Parks was the secretary of the Montgomery, Alabama, chapter of the NAACP.

Forced to the Back

One of Montgomery's Jim Crow laws made it illegal for Black people to sit in the first four rows on a public bus. They had to sit in the back, and if the bus was full, give up their seat to a white passenger. The resulting Montgomery bus boycott lasted a little over a year. The Montgomery bus system lost between 30,000 and 40,000 bus fares every day during the boycott.

Rosa Parks, shown here with Martin Luther King Jr. in the background, later said, "People always say that I didn't give up my seat because I was tired, but that isn't true. I was not tired physically . . . No, the only tired I was, was tired of giving in."

The Montgomery bus boycott lifted King into a public leadership role. But that meant he was targeted by those who didn't want change. King regularly received threats and was arrested during the boycott. On January 30, 1956, the King family home was bombed. King was away organizing the boycott and no one was hurt, but it was a terrifying moment for King, his wife Coretta, and their oldest child, Yolanda.

LOOKING BACK

Today, the bus on which Rosa Parks refused to give up her seat can be found at the Henry Ford Museum in Dearborn, Michigan.

In June 1956, a U.S. court ruled racial segregation on buses was unconstitutional in the case *Browder v. Gayle*. The U.S. Supreme Court upheld the decision in November. The Montgomery bus boycott ended in December 1956. King said, "We came to see that, in the long run, it is more honorable to walk in dignity than ride in humiliation." In 1957, King helped found the Southern Christian Leadership Conference, of which he was elected president.

King met with an angry group of men looking for revenge on his behalf. He wouldn't allow violence in response to the attack. "If you have weapons, take them home," he said. "If you do not have them, please do not seek them. We cannot solve this problem through violence. We must meet violence with nonviolence."

Rosa Parks takes the bus after the Montgomery bus boycott ends in a victory.

Led by King, the Southern Christian Leadership Conference (SCLC) organized the action of protest groups throughout the South, calling on Black churches for support. The SCLC led more nonviolent protests, such as sit-ins at restaurants where Black people weren't allowed to eat. Protestors would often be arrested, sprayed with fire hoses, or beaten by police officers, but King stressed the protestors should never answer with violence.

"The end of violence or the aftermath of violence is bitterness," he said in the speech "The Power of Nonviolence" from 1957. "The aftermath of nonviolence is **reconciliation** and the creation of a beloved community. A boycott is never an end within itself. It is merely a means to awaken a sense of shame within the oppressor but the end is reconciliation, the end is **redemption**."

LOOKING BACK

A sit-in is a nonviolent protest in which people stay in an area and refuse to leave until their demands have been met.

Always Watching

Despite King's nonviolent approach to the civil rights fight, some people thought he was dangerous because he had the support of so many. In late 1963, the Federal Bureau of Investigation (FBI) opened a file on King and closely followed the minister. They listened to his phone calls and had undercover agents watch him for signs of illegal activities. The FBI watched King closely until the day he died.

This photo shows a sit-in at a lunch counter in Durham, North Carolina, in 1960.

IMPRISONED

King was arrested 29 times during the civil rights movement. Even while in jail, he tried to rally support and make people aware of racial injustice. In April 1963, he was jailed for protesting in Birmingham, Alabama. In his "Letter from Birmingham City Jail," King wrote, "We must use time creatively, in the knowledge that the time is always ripe to do right." King knew his cause couldn't wait for him to get out of jail, and his letter proved to be a powerful tool in the fight for civil rights.

POLICE DEPT
BIRMINGHAM ALA

LOOKING BACK

When he was jailed, King was in Birmingham, Alabama, as part of the SCLC's Birmingham Campaign. It was meant to spotlight inequality in the city.

Willing to Sacrifice

President John F. Kennedy expressed support for King during his time in jail, calling Coretta King who was at home with their children. Kennedy was shot and killed in Dallas months later, in November 1963, and many say King expected more violence against himself as well. Speaking at a march in Detroit on June 23, 1963, King said, "If a man has not discovered something that he will die for, he isn't fit to live."

"Injustice anywhere is a threat to justice everywhere," he wrote. King wrote as a response to several religious leaders who had been critical of him and the other protestors. King and other civil rights leaders began to plan a massive rally.

A bomb was thrown at the hotel where Martin Luther King Jr. had been staying in Birmingham, Alabama. King had already left, though other people were injured.

On August 28, 1963, more than 260,000 people gathered on the **National Mall** in Washington, D.C., as part of the March on Washington for Jobs and Freedom. Several civil rights organizations, including the SCLC, had planned the assembly to gather support for civil rights legislation.

Martin Luther King Jr. gave his famous "I Have a Dream" speech. Millions watched on television as he said: "I have a dream that one day this nation will rise up, live out the true meaning of its creed: 'We hold these truths to be self-evident, that all men are created equal.'. . . I have a dream that my four little children will one day live in a nation where they will not be judged by the color of their skin but by the content of their character."

A Call for Freedom

King asked for true freedom, from the "hilltops of New Hampshire" to the "Rockies of Colorado" to the "slopes of California." He cried, "Let freedom ring from Stone Mountain of Georgia . . . and when we allow freedom to ring, . . . [we] will be able to join hands and sing in the words of the old Negro **spiritual**, 'Free at last, Free at last, Thank God A-mighty, We are free at last!'"

LOOKING BACK

King's 17-minute speech is considered one of the best in American history.

I HAVE A DREAM
MARTIN LUTHER KING, JR.
THE MARCH ON WASHINGTON
FOR JOBS AND FREEDOM
AUGUST 28, 1963

An engraving marks the spot where King spoke on the steps of the Lincoln Memorial.

THE NOBEL PEACE PRIZE

In October 1964, Martin Luther King Jr. won the Nobel Peace Prize for his commitment to nonviolence. He received the award in Oslo, Norway, and began his speech by saying, "I accept the Nobel Prize for Peace at a moment when 22 million Negroes of the United States of America are engaged in a creative battle to end the long night of racial injustice."

Dedicating the award to the civil rights movement, King spoke of the resolve his fellow activists felt after the March on Washington: "I accept this award today with an abiding faith in America and an **audacious** faith in the future of mankind." He promised he would "refuse to accept despair" and that he'd keep working for change.

LOOKING BACK

"Negro" and "colored" are words that were once used to label Black Americans that are considered to be offensive today.

Peace Speaker

As the Vietnam War (1955–1975) intensified, King increasingly called for an end to the conflict in speeches and sermons. "As I have walked among the desperate, rejected, and angry young men, I have told them that . . . rifles will not solve their problems," he said in an April 1967 sermon. "But they ask, and rightfully so, 'What about Vietnam?'" King said he couldn't stand by while his government used violence to solve its problems.

At age 35, Martin Luther King Jr. was the youngest person to win the Nobel Peace Prize until Malala Yousafzai won it in 2014 at the age of 17.

LEGISLATION AT LAST

In 1964, President Lyndon Johnson signed the Civil Rights Act. It outlawed segregation in public places, including schools and restaurants, as well as **discrimination** in the workplace. In 1965, Johnson signed the Voting Rights Act into law, which aimed to end laws that kept people from voting. This legislation would not have happened without the work of King, the SCLC, and other civil rights organizations.

"They told us we wouldn't get here," King said in a 1965 speech. "And there were those who said that we would get here only over their dead bodies. But all the world today knows that we are here and we are standing before the forces of power . . . saying, 'We ain't goin' let nobody turn us around.'"

LOOKING BACK

King urged his followers to continue fighting: "I've seen the promised land. I may not get there with you. But I want you to know tonight, that we, as a people, will get to the promised land."

Selma to Montgomery March

Many states were slow to adopt the civil rights legislation. This was the case in Alabama and protestors were met with violence. King and others organized a walk from Selma to Montgomery to support voting rights. March 7, 1965, the day they began, became known as Bloody Sunday. State troopers beat back marchers as horrified Americans watched on television. Hundreds flocked to Alabama to join the march. President Johnson promised to support the bill that became the Voting Rights Act.

King stands behind President Johnson as he signs the Civil Rights Act into law in 1964.

ASSASSINATION

King continued to add his support behind issues affecting Black Americans. In April 1968, he visited Memphis, Tennessee, to encourage **sanitation** workers on **strike** there. On April 4, he was standing on a balcony at the Lorraine Motel when he was fatally shot. He died an hour later. King was 39. A man named James Earl Ray was arrested for the crime 2 months later.

President Johnson called for a national day of mourning on April 7. King's funerals were held on April 9. Thousands attended the two services held in Atlanta, Georgia. King's body was laid to rest in South View Cemetery until his remains were moved in 1977 to what is now the Martin Luther King Jr. National Historic Site.

LOOKING BACK

One of King's last efforts was in support of what was called the Poor People's Campaign, which was meant to address economic injustice in the United States.

A Federal Holiday

After her husband's death, Coretta Scott King and others founded the Martin Luther King Jr. Center for Nonviolent Social Change (later renamed the King Center) in Atlanta, Georgia. She also worked for a national holiday in honor of King. Every third Monday in January is set aside to remember King's legacy of peace and the fight for civil rights in the United States. Many people honor it as a day of service too, helping their communities in different ways.

Martin Luther King Jr. had a private funeral at Ebenezer Baptist Church and a public funeral at Morehouse College.

HOPE OVER DESPAIR

On August 28, 2011, the Martin Luther King, Jr. Memorial opened on the National Mall. King had said during his "I Have a Dream" speech: "This is the faith that I go back to the South with. With this faith we will be able to **hew** out of the mountain of despair a stone of hope." Visitors to the memorial walk through two pieces of granite representing the "mountain of despair" to see a 30-foot (9.1 m) "stone of hope," bearing the image of King. Around the granite structures are engraved 14 of King's quotations about democracy, justice, love, and hope.

King and the civil rights movement brought discrimination and segregation into the public eye. Today, Black Americans and others continue to fight against many forms of injustice. King's legacy remains a guiding influence.

LOOKING BACK

The Martin Luther King, Jr. Memorial opened exactly 48 years after King gave his "I Have a Dream" speech in Washington, D.C.

Continuing the Work

President Barack Obama, the nation's first Black president, spoke at the memorial's opening ceremony. He said: "Nearly 50 years after the March on Washington, our work, Dr. King's work, is not yet complete. We gather here at a moment of great challenge and great change.... And so on this day, in which we celebrate a man and a movement that did so much for this country, let us draw strength from those earlier struggles."

A Timeline of Martin Luther King Jr.

1929 — Martin Luther King Jr. is born Michael King Jr. on January 15.

1934 — King's name is changed to Martin Luther King Jr.

1944 — King begins Morehouse College at age 15.

1948 — King graduates from Morehouse with a degree in sociology.

1951 — King receives a degree from Crozer Theological Seminary.

1953 — King marries Coretta Scott.

1954 — King becomes pastor at Dexter Avenue Baptist Church in Montgomery, Alabama.

1955 — King is a leader of the Montgomery bus boycott.

1963 — King delivers the "I Have a Dream" speech in Washington, D.C.

1964 — The Civil Rights Act is passed; King wins the Nobel Peace Prize.

1965 — The Voting Rights Act is passed.

1968 — King is shot in Memphis, Tennessee, on April 4.

1983 — Martin Luther King Jr. Day becomes a national holiday.

2011 — Martin Luther King, Jr. Memorial opens in Washington, D.C.

GLOSSARY

audacious: Willingly taking a bold risk.

boycott: The act of refusing to have dealings with a person or business in order to force change.

civil disobedience: The breaking of a law as a form of nonviolent protest to force change.

Confederate: Having to do with the Confederate States of America (the Southern states) during the American Civil War.

discrimination: Different—usually unfair—treatment based on factors such as a person's race, age, religion, or gender.

hew: To cut or carve something from stone or wood.

National Mall: A park in Washington, D.C., which is home to many monuments.

reconciliation: The ending of a conflict.

redemption: The saving or improving of something in a poor state.

sanitation: The process of keeping places free from dirt and disease.

segregated: Having to do with the forced separation of races or classes.

sociology: The study of the origin, development, and structure of societies and the behavior of individuals and groups.

spiritual: A religious song, especially one with African American origins.

strike: A refusal to work until changes are made in a workplace.

FOR MORE INFORMATION

Books

Calkhoven, Laurie. *Martin Luther King Jr.* New York, NY: DK Publishing, 2019.

Platt, Christine *A. Martin Luther King Jr.: Fighting for Civil Rights.* New York, NY: Random House, 2020.

Wittenstein, Barry, and Jerry Pinkney. *A Place to Land: Martin Luther King Jr. and the Speech That Inspired a Nation.* New York, NY: Holiday House, 2019.

Websites

Freedom's Ring: King's "I Have a Dream" Speech
freedomsring.stanford.edu/
Hear King give his famous speech on this site.

The King Legacy
www.thekinglegacy.org/content/king-years
Read a detailed timeline of King's life and legacy.

MLK Day
www.americorps.gov/newsroom/events/mlk-day
Find out how you can help others on Martin Luther King Jr. Day.

Publisher's note to educators and parents: Our editors have carefully reviewed these websites to ensure that they are suitable for students. Many websites change frequently, however, and we cannot guarantee that a site's future contents will continue to meet our high standards of quality and educational value. Be advised that students should be closely supervised whenever they access the internet.

INDEX